Feeling Angry

by Rochelle Nielsen Barsuhn
illustrated by
Kathryn Hutton

THE CHILD'S WORLD

ELGIN, ILLINOIS 60120

62

3872

Distributed by Childrens Press, 1224 West Van Buren Street, Chicago, Illinois 60607.

Library of Congress Cataloging in Publication Data

Barsuhn, Rochelle Nielsen, 1958-
  Feeling angry.

  (What's in a word?)
  Rev. ed. of: Angry. ©1982.
  Summary: Presents several situations that can cause
anger, and suggests positive outlets for anger in
helpful, rather than harmful, actions.
    1. Anger—Juvenile literature.   [1. Anger.
2. Emotions]   I. Hutton, Kathryn, ill.   II. Title.
III. Series.
BF575.A5B37   1983   152.4   82-19911
ISBN 0-89565-244-7

4 5 6 7 8 9 10 11 12 R 89 88 87 86 85 84

Angry—Being mad; feeling resentment.
Being upset at someone or some thing.

Sometimes I disagree with my friends.
We shout and fight and hurt each other.
Then I feel sad.

When I stop being mad
and make things right with my friends,
I feel happy.
So do they.

It's better to make people laugh
instead of cry.

When someone is mean to me,
I GET ANGRY

Bullies are mean.
They knock me down.
They push me on the ground
and run.

I cry.
I yell, "You dumb-dumb!"
and chase them.
When I catch one,
I'll push him in the snow
and run.

But then
I'll be a dumb-dumb too.

Lydia promised
to play with me.

But when recess came,
she went to climb the jungle gym
with Ellen.
"You promised!" I said.

But Lydia and Ellen
are hanging by their knees
from the jungle gym.
And I'm angry,
swinging by myself.

Sarah broke
the golden crayon I used
to color rings, kings, and rainbows.

She's not sorry.
She thinks it's funny.

I don't.
I want to break
something of hers.

Instead,
I breathe deeply.

"Sarah," I say, "I'm angry."

Sometimes when things
don't go my way,
I GET ANGRY

"Pick up
 those paints
  before you play."

I knew Grandpa meant what he said.

"But Andrea's here.
 You said I could play."

Grandpa looked at me, shaking his head.

I went to the bedroom
to pick up the paints.

I was mad,
but I did what he said.

As I set up the game
to play again,
Mom said, "It's time for bed now."

I was
    a little
        tired, but . . .
I wanted to play, not sleep!

I felt like crying.
Instead, I hollered
    from the top of the stairs,
"I don't like bed,
    and I don't like you."
Then Mom was angry too.

She came upstairs
and talked with me.
"Sorry I was mean," I said.

It's raining
big splashing drops
even though the whole grade
packed chips and sandwiches
for our spring picnic.

It's no one's fault,
but I want to yell and shout.
Rain spoils picnics.

Lunch is at noon
but I'm hungry now.
That soggy breakfast cereal I ate
won't get me through jump rope
        and cardboard forts.
It makes me angry
that I have to wait.
"I can't!" I say to Mom.
My voice growls like my stomach . . .

        LUNCH!

        Funny how
        after the first bite
        of peanut butter
        the world seems better,
        and I don't growl.

Mom and Dad left
Randall in charge.
Randall's my brother.
He's older.

Randall wanted to watch TV—
a very, very,
        long, long,
                old, old
                        movie.
He wouldn't even listen
to what I wanted to do.

"I'm going to tell,"
I said and shut the door
on Randall
and the TV.

When I don't do what I should,
OTHERS GET ANGRY

Today I watched cartoons
and didn't clean my room.

Dad is angry
because there's dust
and one half-eaten Twinkie under my bed.
I'd rather watch Bugs Bunny
than clean, but
I pick up my toys
and make the bed
and throw that Twinkie in the garbage.
"Dad," I say, "I'm sorry."

Now cartoons will be more fun
and so will Dad.

I made fun of Marvin.
Marvin has mumps.
"You look like a chipmunk," I laughed.
(I saw one once.
Its cheeks were stuffed with nuts.)

But Marvin didn't laugh.
"I do not!" he said.
He frowned at me from his bed,
piled high with toys
and our grey cat.

I didn't mean to make him mad,
so
I brought him ice cream.

When I'm not happy with myself,
I GET ANGRY

My sister's hair is curly.
Mine's straight.
She's good at everything,
even art.

Everyone likes her pictures.
So I get angry
when I can't draw
mud-brown horses like she can.

When I tell Dad,
he smiles.
"You're better in math.
Besides,
your hair is thick
and a beautiful black!"

Today feels rainy-gray
to me
because I'm angry.

I'd rather for the day
to feel sunshiny-yellow.
Then I could do cartwheels
on the grass,
shouting, "Hip, hip, hooray!"

Maybe I should do cartwheels anyway.
They'd help me forget I'm mad.
Then the color of my day would change.
Yes, maybe it's time for a cartwheel.

About the Author:

Rochelle Nielsen Barsuhn studied English literature at Bethel College (St. Paul, Minnesota). Her written work has appeared in several magazines for children. Ms. Barsuhn describes herself as "a reader of books—children's, the classics, and anything in print." Currently, she works with her husband in their Minneapolis-based design and advertising agency.

About the Artist:

Kathryn Hutton graduated from Berea College in Kentucky and attended the Cincinnati (Ohio) Art Academy. She has been a commercial artist for 40 years. Mrs. Hutton particularly likes to draw children and through the years she has used her four children and four grandchildren for inspiration. She resides in "non-retirement" in Fairfield, Ohio.